Voices in the House

Alabama Poetry Series

GENERAL EDITORS: Chase Twichell and Thomas Rabbitt

SUSAN SNIVELY

Voices
in the House

The University of Alabama Press
Tuscaloosa and London

Copyright © 1988 by
The University of Alabama Press
Tuscaloosa, Alabama 35487
All rights reserved
Manufactured in the United States of America

Library of Congress Cataloging-in-Publication Data

Snively, Susan, 1945–
    Voices in the house.

    I. Title.
PS3569.N5V65   1988   811'.54   87-25471
ISBN 0-8173-0393-6
ISBN 0-8173-0394-4 (pbk.)

British Library Cataloguing-in-Publication Data is available.

for my parents

Acknowledgments

My thanks to the National Endowment for the Arts for a fellowship which helped me complete this book, and to the directors of the Bread Loaf Writers' Conference for a fellowship.

Some of the poems in this collection appeared originally in the following journals:

The Georgia Review
"To an Artist Going Blind"

The Kenyon Review
"Soldier and Laughing Girl"
"The Law of Gravity"

The Massachusetts Review
"Masters," "Light of the World," and "What Mystery" in the sequence "Four Poems for Brontë and Dickinson"
"Mary, Queen of Scots"
"Haply I Think on Thee"

Poetry East
"Forgiveness"
"The Wish"
"Music Deepens the Distance"
"After Anger"

The Yale Review
"The Women at the Watching"

Yankee
"Dodge Elegy"

"The Dream Quilt" was published in an anthology of poems, *The Bewildering Thread,* edited by Ruth Mortimer and Sarah Black, published by the ELM Press, Wallingford, Pennsylvania, as part of a special edition by Enid L. Mark.

Contents

Voices in the House

Derby Day

Everyone today is a prize three-year-old,
glossy, imperishable.
               The sun shines bright
on an old familiar goodbye blindness—
your face, hard-edged, already set in gear
for a fast leap ahead, looks back at me
distractedly for what will be the last time.

Horses, socialites, juleps . . . in Kentucky,
my old unlonged-for home far away,
a day to tell stories. Last year's victor, Swale,
five weeks a winner, suddenly dead of nothing.
I am alive in the bloom of television,
part of the mob daydreaming in the sun,
although unblessed by whiskey.
                         It is a year
since I saw you. What more can a mover know?

The horse that wins this year, ridden by Angel,
streaks out in front and stays, arrogant wild boy,
five lengths ahead at the last. I made no bets
but I wouldn't have minded losing just to find
how hard a racing heart will go to win.
As usual at the end I'm breathing fast,
under my hand my heart knocks. New allegiance
seems to have kept a home in me a long time
although, watching the race, I'd only thought
of horses, horses. So do these moments move me

1

I know I don't have to let anything go,
not anything, if only because they run,
the gorgeous dumb hot creatures—for all their
    speed
and all the coinage of sweat spent on them
spread to a glistening by the wind they pass
    through—
like all lovers, to a destined finish.

Forgiveness

Space makes all things possible.
Time's sidecar is packed with stars.
When I am most awake
I wish sleep to drop upon all those
weary chasing names in a black book.
To cease this cold pursuit
leaves room for belief in breath,
the fall that must rise
toward a whisper of sense,
the agitation of aliveness
spinning all things.

The movable grass
springs up after two risen bodies.
See, there is no harm done.
Bones of fingers glow in the leaves.
The mind, lighter than fire,
may open every hour it owns.

The View from Dickinson's

Warts on their necks are not their fault,
no more than hearts of blue quartz.
Still it gives pleasure, from this high
cupola, the ledge fringed with flies,
to watch the wind push citizens around
like stalks of grain, lumpy heads
swaying over the ground they're stuck to.

No wonder one makes friends among the voiceless
until the click of the bat, fly-rasp,
the bee's sweet snores make opera
roll through panes the sunset sharpens.
How easy then to wait for the message,
to face the only trustable thing, the mountains,
with night so complete and death so friendly.

The Chimney Fire

Listen. It raves
in the middle distance
past the oblivious skaters

pushing bombs with sticks,
past the greasy cackle
of the singed pig,

the soft push of boots in snow,
dog-snuffle, bird-caw.
A house is burning inside out,

chimney smoke a tense parabola
above the melting roof,
a box where a blind giant

beats the walls.
One brave neighbor climbs
up to tamp the flue,

another hurries,
his whole body bent forward
in pain against the brake of snow—

how slow his footsteps!—though
he is doing all he can
with the brief strokes he was given.

His heartbeats knot in his legs
as if he were a called dog
working his body

against the little time left.
So unlike the raven,
all spread wing and sharpness

aiming its purpose elsewhere,
head full of air,
or the child watching the pig

blacken as fire
smothers its hide.
(She tastes her fingers

sucked to the bone.)
So unlike the hunters
whose work is over

(or beginning), as dawn pried open
shows the day done for,
a cooked hare.

Lives might vanish
if the roof goes;
then the cold children

hunched at pond's edge,
their heads lifted at the shout of collapse
pinning back a hole in the sky,

would start to run
as they feel the lash
on houses now softly limned

with snowlight, on slim trees,
the cart of winter wheat.
How frail the hands, the feet

that keep so busy,
the huddled roofs
provisional as birds' nests,

where a fire's temper
swiftly crazes
the air's dry stir.

Listen. He stops his hand,
a wind blows through a hole
in the canvas. Can it be

that the fire he started
he cannot finish?
Or will a larger wind,

sprung from glacial hills,
punish these determined lives,
menace the rescue?

The painter regards the mountains,
frowning, heavy-browed,
whose omnipresent weight

matches his sight
with equal power.
The world urged forth by each,

human and mountain,
pushed upward by expressive need,
is riddled with fractures.

As he holds his brush
above the wavering smoke
he wants to believe

each shivering crack
a gift of nature.
Water or trees might fill them

as the cracks in a burning log
fill with eager heat
hastening to break forth.

In this moment
the finished and unfinished
hold in consonance

all acts of love
where one beautifully labors
to ease the other,

moving in dreamy succession
through seasons arching toward sun.
He blows on his fingers:

how many branches,
stark or fervently leaved,
have sprung on pollarded trunks?

The risk of making stiffens his bones.
Nothing he works at
can change this world,

so vulnerable, so cold before his eyes,
although when he sleeps
his teeth champ coarse bread

and the hairs on his head
rise like young stalks
or birds tuned to advancing light.

Faultlines

Something whispers *you don't belong here*
through the new crack in the wall.
The dentist smiles,
his hook in a patch of tar,
saying the pain will stop when the tooth splits.

Houses are made, like people,
for the face to fall.
A hundred years only measure the difference
between the still-warm, hopeful brick
and loosening, redundant mortar.

Souls live among the layers,
fly up on wings barely visible,
grateful, exposed to the air.

"Awake!" Cries the Watchman

Say that there's no use
revisiting old pain,
that's only an excuse.
Reason cannot restrain
the echo of her voice.
Her dying voice speaks plain:
"I'll speak to you again."

In fact she never did.
I never called her back,
aghast at what I'd heard,
a life stretched on a rack,
thin rattle of the dead.
And still it makes me sick
I never called her back.

I know now what I know,
that I was asking her
to let me let her go,
to make it easier.
But knowledge will not do.
My fearful character
stands firmly insecure.

Though otherwise remains
of who we were, and more,
to speak of circumstance
formality forswore

I have to take the chance
mere words will not ensure
stirred water can come clear.

"I'll speak to you again."
So careful with her speech,
indeed she must have known
how far those words would reach
long after she was gone.
Be mindful whom you teach
The night is near. Keep watch.

To an Artist Going Blind

The first sign, confusion of colors.
From now on, blue makes a shiver,
red a taste on the bitten tongue,

yellow the snap of the windowshade
rattling light into your straining face.
All your images are a parade

going by the house for the last time.
You remember concerts: sitting
with your arm around your husband's chair,

his silence and yours peaceable, apart,
each with its mixture of shapes and words—
his words a language not yours,

your colors he could not identify.
Still the arm stayed, and later he held it,
a branch on the rocky drop of a cliff,

when there was no reason not to die
except that he lived and had made life.
What if your life were a lump of clay

whose meaning, like his face in sleep,
wakened finally to your touch?
Now as the sun goes behind buildings,

its hot tattoo gradually muffled,
there is no answer for this darkness
except that your life is in your hands

and you know it the way you knew him
when he spoke to you first in your own language,
the loved words coming on like lights.

Hard Prayers at the
St. Elisabethkirche

Cramped, locked at the knees,
my puffy coat an immovable wedge
between me and my companion,
I can't change position
to fit words to the cold air.
But hardness is an answer;
like fatigue, it tells me
every purpose has its blindness,
love is not light.
When I peer into the shrine
where a reliquary's wedding-cake ivory
crusts bones with nervous beads, my head
seems too big to let me look in.
I am a lapsed Presbyterian Gulliver
in a land of tiny miracles
and for not even the least of these—
say, a quick healing
of my friend's botched mind—
do I qualify.

We are winter animals,
or loaves of bread damped after chilly rising.
Far up, another life goes on
of birds in dusty spaces
under the rooftree, a life so simple
it makes madness, the trick knot
on a wasted skein,
look like vanity.

Later, remembering my bruised knees,
I will know that I stayed
in attentive inertia
(the breathing
of the one beside me
packed with anger)
only a fool would have called courage,
as if watchfulness could help
one so determined to be damned.

A saint's life:
not to be distracted
by the node where bones join flesh,
or flesh the perishing spirit;
and after death, the reward,
an endless supply of healing parts,
multiple pelvises and digits
scattered across Europe like shards of the True
    Cross.
Yet the faithful don't worry;
they leave the mind out of it
since it only drags them down
or out into the street
where each step across invisible ice
risks a breakage
as week by week, reason's wires rip.

Masters

To forbid me to write to you, to refuse to answer me, would be to tear from me my only joy on earth, to deprive me of my last privilege—a privilege I never shall consent willingly to surrender.

Charlotte Brontë to M. Constantin Heger,
November 18, 1845

Master—if it is . . . small eno' to cancel with her life . . . she is satisfied—but punish . . . dont banish her—shut her in prison, Sir—only pledge that you will forgive—sometime—before the grave, and Daisy will not mind—She will awake in . . . your likeness.

Emily Dickinson to "recipient unknown,"
early 1862 (?)

Here is Bernini's statue of St. Theresa,
her mouth open and loose, her head thrown back,
the marble of her lips seeming to sweat
with dew from a hidden vein, as if he'd given her
the kiss of mortal knowledge.
                              What do I know?
The card in the stereopticon doubles its image.
Now she seems no saint, but a stricken woman
with a hidden twin who imitates her movements,
a phantom in a mirror. My headache returns,
legacy of those days I was nearly blind
and wrote forbidden things in the half-darkness,
my pencil like a cane on the slippery page,
leaving a gasping space.
                    Oh, did I offend it—
Her half-closed backward eyes behold her mind.
Why do I need to look? I know her stone
as if it were my flesh and I were caught,
like her, at the moment when she turned to marble.

The post-boy comes. He takes away my letter
and leaves behind a packet of blank paper,
the ream we ordered. *T'girls are up to something*
the blind will see in time. I watch the boy
go down the hill—shoulders, then head quite gone,
my words gone begging with him, asking leave
to write what I have written and write again
six months from now. Buried, your letters rot
in yellowed silk. When the wind rakes the heather
I feel the tree-roots groan and claw the paper.
The mindless earth keeps us.
                                              How can I endure
if I make no effort to ease my sufferings?
In a month or two, how will he answer the question,
smoking alone at his desk in the busy city?
You sit too long at work. You need the air,
jerk of the puppet-string. I felt my lips
strain at their silence; his were closed, turned down,
my eyes could lift that far. His would not hold mine.

Nothing comes over the hills and I go to meet it,
ghost of a letter, ghost of a man in black
whose voice might break from me at any moment
like the rattle of hoof-taps on an icy road.
It is not apparent that I have stopped believing
in time. Beginning and ending are the same
to the one who sits on a rock at a bend in the road
hearing the hoof-taps louder, ever louder,
and closer and here and gone and far away. . . .
Almost too dark to see. Here is my hand.
I hold it out in the moonlight, remove the glove,

unbend the fingers. Cold. When they stop shaking
the wind will die down and I shall go inside
to inscribe the words I need on the face of
   blankness:
the story of one who worshiped the horizon.

Eurydice

Longing streamed from my eyes
through the black lace
veil of my bridal.
When you turned your back
I knew my place.

But which man had assigned
my footsteps, and on which path
toward the world's end—
music of earth
or winter death?

A king's hands on my head
crowned me, let go;
by such an act
I knew he understood
what I came to know,

that sorrow hides the choice
I made to turn away
from you, who would keep me
listening to your voice.
But though death eats the day

his heart is deep
for knowing how love tires
of looking after life
as at the wild stars
that never sleep.

The Cutting Edge

I

Driving elaborate patterns in a parking lot,
I avoid the man standing and waiting,

his hands stiff with apology.
He stands there like a metal garbage can

ringing with voices of schoolkids, trash goodbyes.
An angry woman rides the air between us.

She owns a name we would never violate
but her jealous dreams are a joke trap,

an engine with ravening wheels
where we all have fallen.

Years later, when I try the silence
with a birthday greeting in a sunlit moment,

he will wave me away,
beggar refusing beggar.

II

Another love. The engine spun quietly,
tuned to deeper modulations

as my voice stilled
in the dense river of another's need.

In the car with me, he would sleep
while my right foot pressed down

as if to soft-pedal a piano.
But in fact I never played for him.

Seeing how he loved only excellence,
I hid my weak left hand, my botched dynamics.

How I loved it when he confessed a weakness,
the beautiful words hastening like rain

into a golden basin
where even poison might leave no trace.

But madness kept changing the faces
we turned toward each other.

The side I left open to fusion
became the cutting edge of my complaint

at how love could ruin itself.
Proverbs of blame whistled thin voices

from an airless room behind the wallpaper
and through the blades of the window fan.

III

A future doubled over on the past
awakens slowly in darkness,

uneasily moves numb feet
to test a truculent shoal.

Daylight asks for a clenched fist,
a face to practice strength.

But when the alarm ceases
I drift in a wordless telepathy

of sad photographs.
His face rises to me

from the bottom of a pool.
Flat leaves loosen from his hair

like the scales of a disintegrating crown,
and his hair floats free, stirred by the wind,

a breath among currents.
Look cannot answer look,

the moment is free of questions.
To keep each hour an upturned palm,

as the heavy day stretches,
is all I can do

with a small, provisional faith.
In time, light will rhyme on the hills

of a valley preparing for sunset,
traffic slowing before evening rush,

here and there in an emptying building
a mind caught in an unexpected dream

whose borders are soft now, almost permissive,
although distance never lets them disappear.

Poem on Her Birthday

Last year the smell of gardens
rose around us, while the concert player
released your heart of its chimera.

Perfectly strange, the hand I held
while the music suddenly turned
into the assault of mutual need

bearing such a weight
we could only hold it by keeping
our eyes turned toward each other.

Now only metaphor sweetens a mourning voice,
although losing is a kind of having
and the new year less radiant than clear.

The Law of Gravity

I

If I shut my eyes, everything I remember
slides by on its heavy barge
low in the water, voices a fleet mockery

of lights on the muddy river.
In the valleys of the Neckar
heat is a stone with live, sputtering veins.

You are a drowning man I cannot save
from the undertow
deranging your cargo of labor.

Your angry voice is the god of these deeps,
your words gray clouds
thunderous, obdurate,

heavy over the Rheinplain
simmering in its humid wastes
of agoraphobic yellow-green.

I run away north the way the river runs
past all the freight it can bear.
Holland's weather enlarges the air of Europe;

blue upon blue
gives a sense of permission,
opens my hope.

II

Beside a wide brown field of peat
my friend Jeanne, who lives in this studio,
talks in Dutch to a neighbor.

The letter *h* curls in the air between them
like the moist pock of a shovel sunk in earth.
Their words rise, then fall,

fronds and tentacles intact,
taking root in the land they came from
while voices pedal away into far thunder.

Far off the traffic turns the noise to light.
How easy right now simply to breathe
the beautiful purple and dark blue

as time opens a moment
to brim and shimmer
before it hardens and scuttles away.

The storm we are all watching
comes on slowly.
Blue thunderheads build,

the sunset bursts through
thick bars of back-lit cloud
as the North Sea rides in,

its vanguard of small boats
tugging the big blind ship
noisy with scurrying minions.

III

Once I thought you and I
were the bride and groom in a Chagall painting.
Our horses stepped lightly in the air

where blue was not the color of storms
nor of the cloak of reason
but of the wedding night where all is permitted.

On canvas the figures rise up,
the flaming cloud suspended in pink
holds the eight seconds of sunset

as an eternity.
Such visions, even whispered
into the seething design of our fantasy

would start an invisible crack
in the lapis lazuli,
a sidelong startle in the rapt profile.

Yet I reach for you across the distance,
the white page of faint consolation,
and watch my hand trying to open itself.

It holds me to the earth
even when my face is set seawards
toward the only country I belong in;

it is why I return to wait out the summer
for no other reason
than the moist hands' need

for disintegrating clay
to fill up their emptiness
with the humblest substance.

IV

Darkness takes the house away.
I do not notice the storm has cleared off
until the wind ceases to smell like salt

and smells again like fish from the lake.
The letter *h* has softened
to *s* and farewell. Forms recede,

lights take their place.
On her canvas Jeanne is daubing
a quick succession of yellow-green dots,

regular but crooked, like stars.
In the end I talk to you simply,
only of things that once gave us joy.

Now the air can fill up
with the earthy talk of woman and woman,
laughter weighted by regret,

regret lightened by laughter.
My friend makes a long brushstroke
with clear furrows of light and dark

which trail land across the horizon.
Paint in the capable hand of the painter
returns earth to evening.

Somehow the sky too has come down here
in the colors of crushed precious stone—
a beautiful sign,

a word, a look.
There is no way to tell you this
as if it could restore our lives.

We do not know where the center is
in which we might feel held and calmed
yet keep ourselves wakeful.

Only at times, unlooked-for,
the sky slips downward through
the sealed vault we knock our heads against,

letting us lift off and let go,
an arc of light and color
wordless as two bodies turning

together across space,
the air between earth and sky
released to the work of their hands.

Light of the World

At night I am a match for everything.
If I walk down the street
I may go invisible
toward the hulk of the church
where the cold beggar sleeping in its porch
can see by my corona
the weather of his hands.

I remember your blessing my head;
patriarch, lover of words,
you stopped your touch an inch above the hair
whose color, you said, shed flame.
Through my scalp I could feel
the warmth, the trembling.
Always I am just that much apart
from the triumphant rise or fall.

The sun, with its big white eye, sees me,
my whole body an arrow tipped with diamond.
Such exposure I have kept to myself,
withheld the light, measured it out,
to print the dark with stars.
In another world my eyes would grow accustomed.
Here, I carry brightness on my shoulder,
going out alone in the raw spring
to see the water gradually deepen,
its black cataract engrave the earth.

Mud Mask Pantoum

When the dead king's long gone under
diatoms start to crack the face.
My secret double wants to dance;
she's ready for the earth to move.

When diatoms start to crack the face
it's like a rain of splatters in the oven;
the meat's ready to make its move
in the lives of ruddy, salty cells.

Like a rain of splatters in the oven,
tears run free behind the mask;
in the lives of ruddy, salty cells
aging sits down to eat with hunger.

Do tears run free? Behind the mask
each splayed pore shuts quickly up.
Aging sits down to eat too hungry
for love to keep the face up tight.

Each splayed pore shuts quickly up.
It's ugly to cry a whole day's drizzle
for love. To keep the face uptight
I hide under puff-adder paste

but a laugh's as good as gold. Why dazzle
a dead king long gone under?
Age is a dry puff-adder. Taste
your secret double. Want to dance?

Provençal Rooster

The five notes say it plain:
love is hot, hard work.

What if his cry were the conscience
of a world not French—
starchy, acidic,
where no soft dawn mellows the night's leavings?

Oh, but those sweet shadows talk like waves
and our big dreamy boat goes gently,
all its couples peaceable
as long as they ride.

Board Game of Provence

Who thinks of money, the New World's charm and
    penalty,
magic pieces so cleverly mobile
they roll over mountains at a foot's touch?
Narcotic with color, tastes
of old surprises pique the tongue:
what is it, can we see it from here,
what will our lives be like in paradise?

Bible Salesmen in Rural France

Why not, in the Saturday morning light,
greet the two pale men who have walked so far
into the scrub oak and *jeunesse,*
by spending three francs for a book
that shows how to live happily forever?
Their faces, the color of puff pastry,
bend eagerly above the gluey pastels
where everyone looks well-fed and Polynesian.
How to live? Someone makes tracks on a map
toward the hope of a palm crossed with silver;
another dreams in a space cleared by the sun
but for the olive branch, its tense monochrome.

Typing with the Nuns

Under the keys, Mozart is trying to sleep
while we punch letters out of his minuets.
For a treat, we get Haydn's "Surprise"
when the carriages slam on the triple *forte*.

There are no screens. The flies cruise around,
soulless little lives the sister ignores
as she overlooks the heat, her wimple a sweat band,
her many layers concealing God knows what.

I am the only Protestant in the class,
out of reach of the holy water
and the Hail Mary, one long word hanging in hot air.
Already I am beginning to burn,

and at thirteen, I bleed any old time.
Ashamed, I ask for help from this woman
with a man's name stuck to her own—Paul or
   Joseph.
How does she know about this flowing?

Her strong fingers pin the stain shut.
Now I can descend to Mother in the boiling car.
Only the sister and I know it is there
like the feel of old apple in the mouth.

Gerstle's Place

"304 is the cow's tail!"
The campers greeted our bus,
late, packed with screamers
and sleepers. Bored already,
I'd head for the "nature trail"
to hunt sharp-tongued sassafras
and scout for Teddy,
the cuter of the Ogle twins,
who loved to say
"You lie like a rug."
Afternoons, I'd haunt the Osage
Indian "camp," a dust-bowl
tamped by cold footprints,
where in the warm, bug-fusty
quiet I felt anonymity
settle in like hunger
after our miniature box lunch.

Home on the cow's tail
(my house a long way
up near the snout)
I would think nothing sadder
than five o'clock summer sun
through cruddy windows,
the smell of chlorine
from a damp suit.
At the same minute each day
we'd pass a bar

with a sign on the door,
No Ladies,
in faded cursive.
No lady yet, barely female,
so hungry I felt barely alive
in the hollow where blood sugar
had ebbed and left me,
I wanted inside:
surely after all,
since they were everywhere,
ladies could sit there.

If the bus smoked and stopped,
if Teddy fetched up sick,
wouldn't Gerstle crack
his dirty door to let us in?
—Years later, strolling that street,
my mother would dig my side,
"Gerstle's! Imagine what sort
go to a place like that;
ptomaine or worse."
(We'd lunch with other ladies.)
What sort of what?—
I rode home with dirty feet
(toe-main), small tired bones
(a bag o' bones), a small belly
so quick to fill and to empty.

Sledding on Lunatic Hill

It's the fifties. Flying Saucers
zoom kids downhill
so zoned-out they think they're on the moon.
The five of us are the same age
except for a little sister, the only one
not crying at this dizzy turnabout.
Stolid, in red boots, she looks at us,
eyes slit in a heavy head
we don't know will grow to adult size
while the rest of her stays six.
I'll never see her cry.
Her grownup's brains stop her mouth
in the age of the not-to-be-mentioned.
Our toes grow cold. We want to go home.
The hospital stares down,
a brown meanness behind the fence.
Think of a whole life in a snowsuit,
breathing through zippers, tasting soup,
our mothers unable to steady their fingers
long enough to help us escape.

The Wish

There was the small soft belly
with me inside, six months done,
and my mother shyly posed
with my father in his Coast Guard uniform.
She said she hardly showed,
("Where are you carrying it, under your arm?")
then, a plunge from crest to trough—
not in there, *not* my mother,
the two of them never started anything
and the war was a phantom also
of fat-headed men, miles of spiked guns
rolling backward into the maws of planes
as ships' raked stacks swallowed their filth. . . .
As if I could flatten it all to paper
crowded with faces, a spinning collage
of everyone shrunken and sickly equal,
I send them all back into darkness
which taking them easily in, grows huger
with noise, books, braggy inventions,
jerk-machinery, horses, flung bones,
a wheel of mad prayer I can't stop
until the stars in Cassiopeia start to bleed,
all because I pushed this button
from boredom, to see what the mind could do
with a single prehistoric photograph
and a blank wish unraveling in the day,
random and cool as clouds, to disappear.

Mary, Queen of Scots

"His lips teased a path from neck to knee."
I read the words again. What lay between
was no man's land to me. I was sixteen.
Bothwell, at Holyrood, had worked his way

into the queen's apartment. With his glove
he slapped her face, then ripped her dress to shreds.
The heavy velvet, gold-encrusted threads
were nothing to a Scotsman hot for love.

I had to hold the book straight up while lying
on my back, the doctor said. My lung
was busted. I felt brave and good and young.
It hurt like hell. At least I wasn't dying,

and so I thought the prayerful delegation
from church could just as well go home and pray
for someone else, leaving me in the fray
where Bothwell, as they say, forgot his station.

The young queen trembled by the curtained bed,
treasures laid open to a wild man who
would make her let him do what he would do.
A mess of swarming images, my head.

There were no words for such a wordless trick.
I lay on my back. Nurses came in and took
my temperature and pried me from the book.
Mercury throbbed along the little stick.

Sight for Sore Eyes

(for my brother)

The hollowfaced ones on *Twilight Zone*
scared you so bad I had to take out the *World Book*
and read you about incendiary bombs.
A thumb in the mouth's OK at seven
if your sister licks garlic butter from a jar.
Daddy's barbecue smoke
didn't get into the den past the air conditioner;
they didn't hear you screaming. I was scared too
the week death took to the road
as a pasty-faced man that reared up over back seats.

Thumb or tongue,
anatomy's a comfort
when you loosen up the arrangements.
Remember the grape-stuffing contest,
twenty in my mouth, twenty-one in yours,
certain death at the wrong end of a laugh?
They rolled into every corner, like BBs,
birdshot, birdseed, as our grins burst.
Maybe one's still there, dry-eyed now,
a puzzle piece we'd both pounce on
to recompose whatever decomposes.

Flu in October

Faces spin
in a yellow pool
stirred by a mean dream.
Quiet, be quiet
until the sky stops.
Now the wheezing school
bus deposits
a lone child,
one seed from a bright pod.
Somewhere the vast, tricky
day-machine twists a valve
to let off an hour's steam,
a trapped laugh flies up.
Leaves hustle
through a silver door
draped with rain.

Talk with the Beast

Some days all poems are footfalls
on the nerves' shaky jelly.
Then metaphor starts up its greasy wheels
to plow one lane clean on a rutted road.
Stop it. I can't. I want to lie down
in a poem I read about a wet lost dog
and make it all up for myself, and better,
the way that poet may have felt
after driving home his fiercest pain.
How will I teach my ghost to go on
by saying not what is but what is like it
when it comes up like an animal, asking?

A Box of Devils Found in a Junk Shop

Disguised as napkin-rings
carved in blood-brown wood,
they gleam in the box,
ten little monkey heads
fitted with torture-teeth,
eyes bulging with malice,
rapine, or wrath,
seven deadlies and three extra
for any new-plucked sin.

Who carved them?
A hater of food and company
likely to fork his tongue
to prod a guest's snug flab,
or one who dined alone
among ghosts of gluttonies
caved into bones?

If, as Scrooge knew,
doorknockers howl, guts churn
nightmares out of bits of suet,
what might one of these do,
watching from across the plate
our busy, fulfilling mouths,
our laps drifted with napery?

No vagrant calories, these,
supplying fuel stored

irretrievably unburned
in drab provinces.
The life of hand-to-mouth,
instantly sinister,
stops cold in mid-air
as the loaded spoon drops.
Rusty knives clack in the skull:
Marley, Mephisto, Belial.

After Anger

Lava poured into the holes of morning
from the night's secret eruptions.

Hardening in the sudden chill
it assumed terrible shapes

the big wind could propel
with its blind shout.

A bird perched on a trembling limb.
It was small and yellow, like its own heart,

but its feet knew no fear.
They clutched and rode,

clutched and rode,
until the shapes wept into black pools.

Now when the bird flies over them
it cannot see its reflection.

It stays awake all night
listening for movement in the stripped branches.

Haply I Think on Thee

Some days it's all there is,
   a sky thin as airmail paper
      and nothing to say. Look

for whatever turns up
   on a heavy train
      aware at every stop

of the whole heartbeat of a crowd.
   A shadowy passage I read
      says a vampire is loose in the city,

an old man freshly immortal
   from his last belovèd kill,
      and trim in his nobleman's black.

He spies a woman in a carriage
   and thinks of breakfast in the palace of her throat.
      Daydreams escort old enemies

into fiction's first-class compartment
   where they hide their smiles behind paper.
      In the double-paned windows

I see my own wavering image,
   the laws of the false mirror
      pulling at the halves of my face.

You by my side, deep in someone's words,
   look through to another world.
      The distraction ennobles you,

gives the elusive intellect
   the cool of your profile.
      Meanwhile I travel sideways,

no more at odds than anyone
   for holding the open book in my hands
      invisible under the print of the remembered.

All Souls' Day

(Brueghel, *The Return of the Herd*)

On All Hallows' Eve, Saint Bertulph, buried at
    Ghent,
knocks on the sides of his coffin
to warn all bones about the battle.
As we move slowly up the dry hill
above the crying vines,
picked bodies whistle on gibbets.
The roots have grown, their fruit is cut down.
When was life ever not labor?

How long has it been since I looked
into the wide eyes of cattle and was forgiven?
We push at their backs with sticks,
shouting their stupidity. A black spirit
watches in a tree
for the storm's iron outriders.
Are we going home or are we going to hell?

The hermit said he heard in his cave,
exhaled through a dark fissure,
a wind filled with bitter voices.
What could a simple sleep do with these,
so many and so hungry?
We clasp our flanks and lie low,
each by each in heavy bodies,
hoping our souls return before strange hands
take up our bones to lay them down forever.

Chinese Puzzle Ball

He picks up a knife
and makes a hole in the ivory
through which he carves
a sphere inside the first sphere
working the curvature
with the scythes of little knives.
He will work on the puzzle every
day, every year of his life

placing the holes geometrically,
stippling their edges
like embroidered eyes.
After the eighth sphere, he can begin
the trees, the mountain dogwood, the women
coming through the garden in threes,
over paths, over bridges
and followed respectfully

by small men carrying fans
tricked with the willow-pattern.
Pale, they seem painted,
and it exhausts you to look,
to think of him working until dark
after the night has taken him, blunted
his knife, and his head is a cavern
littered with filigreed stumps of bones. . . .

Your tongue worries your teeth.
Look—turning—you can see the sky,

no blank, but a promenade
filled with birds. A busy planet
with seven other planets in it
orderly and perfectly made:
women in the gardens in his eye
and his heart, and his heart in his mouth—

for see how this footpath runs
into a line so thin
the blade he held must have come
down once, touched, and come up
again, one slip
an unpardonable crime.
Day after day, the hard place: a man
with a knife, the world in his hands.

Soldier and Laughing Girl

(Vermeer)

How long has the wine slept in her glass?
The painter tells her to stay as she is.
He is interested in the light
her face receives, like a draught
of wine still and clear, or tolerant weather.
Laughter's bright color hides all shadow.

The soldier's posture speaks his pleasure,
elbow out, knee importantly placed,
the black hat a huge statement
whole crowds might gather under.
Who knows it is a man's whole business
to speak against instant apprehension?

Many women have sat as she does,
listening to a history of quick fortune.
What else has she to do but this,
to receive the light like freedom?
It seems a natural breathing,
a smile at the one taking leave.

If she lifted her glass would her face change,
break open to take back its openness,
swallowing her complaisance, to release
tears now mute behind her eyes?
It is so easy to misread her.
A closer look unfastens no mysteries—

no knowledge in the formal arrangement.
The light is just an order her face receives,
the painter's coded, quickening dance.
It is all she can do to shine and smile,
the window before her with the business of day,
a clamor suffered in her balance.

The Women at the Watching

(Hugo van der Goes' Portinari Altarpiece)

Columbine, sorrow; scarlet lily, blood;
iris, the sword empurpled in the heart—
a still life at the border of the picture,
passwords to the adoration.
Someone has come too close, and shaken loose
a spill of blossoms. So must our nerves learn
how life wearies itself to stay intact
in all those fragile, secretive faces. . . .

Outside the circle every mind is troubled,
desperate, formless. Inside, every mortal
suspends himself, arresting breath
to watch this moment gather to perfection
and enter space as a crystal integer
hung among cloudy agitated numbers.
Arrayed but all unready, evil is here
or fear with its armory of teeth and eyes,
a monster hiding in St. Margaret's drapery.
What can a saint do but remain watchful,
seeing how all are invited to this scene?
And yet it must devour her strength to live
in such a world, where even the son of God,
just hours old, looks old before his time.

The fatigue of women is their pondering heart,
the sleep denied in labor for the lord.
Their stretched nerves pulse beneath the mask
of pale gold skin across the hammered bone,

the shaven ivory foreheads. How to bear
the weight of a hundred heart-stopping thoughts?
The frail obedient mother of all mothers,
rising and falling in a sea of blue
about her knees, keeps her eyes cast down.
See what I've done.
What have I done that this should be done to me?

Quiet, so quiet. Wind in the wintry trees
hangs still in early morning. If it blows
secretly in the garments of the angels
it does so for decoration only.
What could the shepherds say, with only gnarled
hands for gesture, straining forward
as if this naked boy could speak?
He is a scrap of light, a golden coal
dropped from an interplanetary fire.
His mother wears out from watching him, yet
   everything
depends on dignity.
                    In this secret kingdom
a traveler in a long footsore parade
might think he hears a cry. But no one offers
a word; whispers have stilled in frozen grass.
Parts of the world are gathered here, and she,
knowing that nothing else is possible,
holds them together with her suffering.

Music Deepens the Distance

Consider the word *no,*
   the most powerful word in the language,
   how far it can travel from the tongue.

So the turning earth keeps losing its edge.
   Or writing a letter, I lose the words
   to the notes my head hears.

How does it feel to write something
   so needful yet so free of time,
   animals opening and closing their mouths

dumbly on the page, but with portent
   a pair of hands could release?
   No, you say, music is not like that,

but you could write that on a flag and fly it
   and I would not understand.
   I am talking about what happens in the mind

when love takes hold. In the pure pain
   a nucleus knows, part of the world
   looks after the changed, fleeting

other part, saying *I can't go with you,*
   every word a million quick cells long.
   At night I listen to the night, opus of loss.

It tells me nothing in the form of everything,
and I learn it and learn it again,
blind player homing on the keys.

Reply to Bad News

Today is a plain day,
sap loosening from the trees,
so much of it drained for just a pound of
    sweetness.
To know these things from the inside
is a life's work.
The tree notices nothing,
a little weak in the feathery upper reaches,
whose background is a faint blue
a grainy sunset will gradually
corrupt to an opulent red.

The Dream Quilt

Here are scraps brought to light.
a long English sunset,
a field with smokestacks, loaves of sheep,

the thoughtful haze of a pipe
and the ruins of a beautiful house
built to fall perfectly

from skylight to newmown grass.
Isn't it a gift how colors blend, inviting
blue-gray, the hue of resolution,

to join trusting brown to unearthly rose?
Love is more secret than a poem is.
I choose to keep the stitchery invisible.

Dodge Elegy

A flatbed for your heap,
the stove-in doors, crazed wheels,
all your worked-over and overworked parts
showing through your sides like the joints of a
    butchered cow. . . .
I watch you ride off,
old friend, old green metal mother
where I rode the waves of eight years,
born out of you again and again,
with each journey across the hills
a little more free, a little more sure where to go.

The times I thought we would die together,
on ice or in pelting darkness,
strafed by semis, runaway along hissing curves—
even then you kept me light of foot,
steady as a lucky heart.
This last year you kept moving
in spite of yourself, your age, and the weather,
like an old lady climbing up to the P.O.
for the letter she does not really expect.

Where the maniac's wagon pushed you to the house,
my husband's car nosed into your side,
a small fish speared to a bigger fish,
deep furrows run with broken glass.
I would believe it's all we're made of
or all that our carelessness leaves behind

but for your courtesy light
working at last,
all night from your wrecked hulk
keeping watch over the lawn's trenches.

Inviting a Friend to Supper

Our fourth, a guest, is witty, a little shy,
and unfamiliar with our fifteen years
packed with old funny stories. And he's attractive.
So I, who can make a buxom chicken dance
in veils of *sauce piquante*, outstrip myself
to keep our mouths moving one way or another.

Dieting radically, you have brought your food.
My stuff is full of *yin* and sinister spices;
one bite of it would snare you in a migraine.
The grand painted balloon of conversation
drifts in the winey air above our heads.
Each keeps it up, letting no air escape,
perfectly balanced between gas and ballast.
Leaning back, sated to quietude,
I feel the ladder of the dining chair
press on my spine, the padded seat grow harder.
Under the plum sauce and the sesame seed,
lemon and parsley, it was just a chicken.

Dessert is a trifle only you decline.
You wonder if I'm battering at your wall,
determined to poison you, perhaps, with sweetness.
Eventually you wish that I were gone,
this interfering hostess, so that you
can talk to men whose interest is your own.
I look into the teacup, where I see
the quavering image of my resident specter.

If I left the table, what would there be between us
but a field where rivals charged and fought for flags?

Digestive cheese and fruit. You watch us nibble,
careless and casual in our home-grown sins,
stacking up calories like poker chips.
The plate under your bowl is clean and shining,
nothing to do but put it away.
Tomorrow you and I will talk of the guest
as if we knew his pith, his disposition,
and the next day you know we'll talk about you.
Knowing how you've interpreted my history
to those who bring the stories back to me,
I dread to overhear what you might say,
although I've kept back more than you could know.

Sounds of a summer night. Horses pass by;
each with its bareback rider keeps its pace
even when Kawasakis rip the streets.
My mouth is full of names. How to stop talking?
I feel like being quiet for a long time
if only to visit, in my mind, a place
where long ago we innocently met.
A tributary of the Thames, at Oxford:
on it a punt in which we sang and paddled
self-consciously aware that we were singing
but trained enough to keep the pitch secure
through Josquin's *Missa Ave Maris Stella,*
star of the sea, which sounds so good on water.
Expert at punting, you would curl your toes
around the lip of the platform as you poled;
the boat held steady even though your voice shook

and I sang louder at those passages
until we arrived at a calm supply of cadence.

This memory makes a quiet hotel, where strangers
can sit and talk or leave each other be
or settle in the lobby after dinner
and read in a corner underneath a lamp
whose fringed shade quivers slightly, stirred by
   breath,
their presence a human comfort in the room
like a long marriage.
             If we were not friends
we could be friends the way such people are
who begin at dinner with some harmless news
of weather and then remark how good the food is,
then start their words edging toward memory,
the strangeness of it beckoning the truth,
their common faults and virtues brought to light,
starting their lives all over: as we might.

What Mystery

To pity those that know her not
Is helped by the regret
That those who know her, know her less
The nearer her they get.

               Dickinson, P. 1400 ("What mystery
               pervades a well")

Behind the daguerreotype, the crayon drawing,
an unknown face shifts her smile,

the eyes and hair shining evidence
you cannot comb or see through.

I am alive in my strange century,
whose litter and crockery you may break

into shards of boredom, derangement,
nothing you can hold out hope in.

Still, my life was complete in its way,
my father's house nearly my own;

in its rooms I breathed a power
which held me when I could not see.

The letters stir in the box,
atom by atom the words give up their spells.

You may touch all my touched objects,
tracing my ephemera in rosewood or horsehair

while the old century sleeps in your own,
its weary battalions fallen against their arms,

its wives and husbands unloosed from whalebone
    and velvet,
sad children roaming in dreams of lizards.

Standing in our rooms you may be moved to tears.
Like us, they will wait for their right time to escape.

Do not think you have found us,
for we are the ones with the privilege of movement:

time that travels the riderless circuits,
lifting and dropping us on breathless wheels—

we knew, even when we were lost,
that it would take us everywhere we wanted to go.

Praise

(for Donald Wheelock)

Sometimes I read like a lake, host to a small
    quick creature who swims in the light
        just under the surface, its feelers

and back seamed with a skein of colors,
    each thread green or yellow, but all
        an unnameable element

of silence and movement. I let it lead me,
    not even calling it poetry,
        it could be animal or love or being.

I imagine you chasing it, critically
    measuring the water's distance to its well
        of oracle or memorial song.

We live with a third one,
    life brimming with words, expansive planet,
        not a child, though if it were we would pay it

equal attention.
    All lives are elegiac, you'd say, seeking
        the fullest source still hospitable.

But purpose falls. Winter air's white water
    sends us spurious fumes, mists;
        we wake in early morning to the dolor

of a mind whose marks are eraser
   dust on the world's reeling scroll.
      It is all we can find to talk about:

take up the blunt recalcitrant pencil,
   sharpen it against self-doubt,
      believe it helps that air changes

so often its key and color. But I wonder
   (and here in the wall I find a door
      with a knob, at my thought, already turning)

I wonder what you would do with the clouds
   I saw yesterday from the car;
      they were of every color clouds

can be, pitched on one another,
   high wind humming and running
      every color together

announcing coldness tomorrow
   or the raw kind of burning
      only a cloud could know.

I wonder what they would do to your sleep's
   dense secrecy.
      That is all I have. Not even shared sorrow,

not anything except a shape changing,
   more change than shape. Nor can I praise the
   weather
      but hope for its largest breath

to draw us in with such capacity
   it comes out poem, song, more breath
      until everything we do is a beginning,

even the running scared under cold air
   among the wind-battered trees
      standing there because they are there.

Voices in the House

All by itself the piano
starts up again.
Or was it cats,
hunting unprintable notes?
Downstairs, my neighbors'
two little girls
turn their faces up to pipe
the impossible treble of youth.
A flight of signals
whisks the surface of the air,
then settles into the staying power
of a tune composed and remembered.
At midnight, when the train comes,
I dream a far friend
stood on an invisible mountain
and woke me out of sleep
with wind from his semaphoring arms.
My fingers unfurl
the music beneath them;
deep in my mind
a rope lets down, a steady thread
probing the well
for an earthly, pure profundity.

Paintwork

While the new blue primer
slaps the gray undercoat,
a radio spits a voice too loud,
rattling the spirit
that dreamed to ease
into work, as into water.

Nothing to do but persist
in the summer's labor,
room by room, to reclaim
an elegance long-lost.
Tender glamour
soothes the dim

wood bitten with scars,
the windows' skimpy sash
too feeble to hold glass,
though the music room floor
(I mean the parlor floor)
is too stained and crazed

to restore as it was when
a wing chair and a rope bed
did for the local pastor
and clean silver sand
or rushes on wide board
made charity homely.

The first strokes brighten,
shudder. Too late
to worry what *they* would think,
ghost or neighbor.
It's ours now, and mine,
a room once dwelled in

by chickens, whose baroque
peckings decorate the door
with an S-curve no saw could make.
I strain to hear whimper and flutter
only half-familiar
here, to a town-dweller.

A friend's voice winds out
of the radio, talking of a poet
he'd put on a dollar bill—
legal tender to annul
her long neglect.
Would she, "half-crack'd,"

agree to be made whole
to be handed about?
I am in a bad mood;
my friend, now exalted,
once given to call
on affairs of the heart

and hear himself out
has disappeared
into his public voice.
Sadly I paint his face

into the window sash
as the afternoon grays.

I'm trying to stay rational
thinking of day's end
when I'll say to my husband
stirring "Williamsburg buff"
in the parlor below,
"Odd, how people

live in the walls,
you'll never guess who turned up."
My mother, famous
for weird dreams, felt a stir here
close to her in the air,
a small breath at her ear.

Could be Submit or Mercy,
wives of a master carpenter
or one of their children—
young Submit, dead early
in the tiny "birthing room"
nearest the huge hearth.

Whose lives is mine kin to?
Surely someone else,
sister or second wife,
has felt, as I often do,
merely provisional
like an extra pair of eyes.

So simple, so changeable,
these strokes, laden
with undercoat, the resin
that makes the blue bearable
to a rough grain long unlaved.
How could I have made ready?

—Myself, I mean. No answer.
I imagine what life there is
left in the walls shaken
like dust into our eyes
so we could hardly see
whether the mirrors give back

old forms in our disguise,
but that's a way of saying
I want, after all, their blessing
on this enterprise,
because I want to bless
the life I chose for me.

No answer. My hand and head
are at least a hundred years
older. I want a clean bed,
the relief of tears
in darkness, like a child's,
and a long swim of sleep.

Dark. The radio's gone quiet.
Cows are in for the night.
I can almost hear the mist
come forth to cover up

all but the plainest shape.
Now that light has passed,

as the carpenter did then
who hoped his house would last,
I put my work down
as all workers must
until light comes again
to show what I have done.